THE ART OF DRAWING
MANGA™
HEROES &VILLAINS

Author: Max Marlborough has been passionate about graphic design and manga from an early age and works as a freelance author, illustrator and designer of art guides for readers of all ages.

Artist: David Antram studied at Eastbourne College of Art and then worked in advertising for fifteen years before becoming a full-time artist. He has since illustrated many popular information books for children and young adults, including more than 60 titles in the bestselling *You Wouldn't Want To Be* series.

Additional artwork: Shutterstock

Published in Great Britain in MMXIX by
Book House, an imprint of
The Salariya Book Company Ltd
25 Marlborough Place, Brighton BN1 1UB
www.salariya.com

PB ISBN: 978-1-912537-58-7

SCRIBO BOOK HOUSE SCRIBBLERS

1 3 5 7 9 8 6 4 2

A CIP catalogue record for this book is available from the British Library.

Printed and bound in China.

Visit
www.salariya.com
for our online catalogue and
free fun stuff.

PAPER FROM

SUSTAINABLE
FORESTS

THE ART OF DRAWING
MANGA™

HEROES
&VILLAINS

BOOK HOUSE
a SALARIYA *imprint*

Contents

Making a start

Introduction

The key to drawing well is learning to look carefully. Study your subject until you know it really well. Keep a sketchbook with you and draw whenever you get the chance. Even doodling is good – it helps to make your drawing more confident. You'll soon develop your own style of drawing, but this book will help you to find your way.

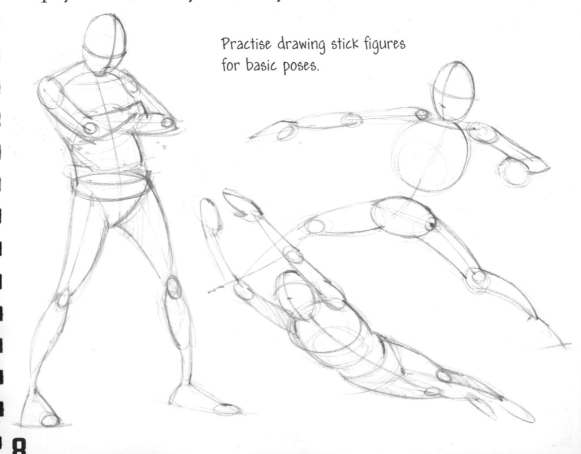

Practise drawing stick figures for basic poses.

Quick sketches

Try sketching
details from books
or magazines.

Introduction (2)

Practise drawing basic head
and body shapes.

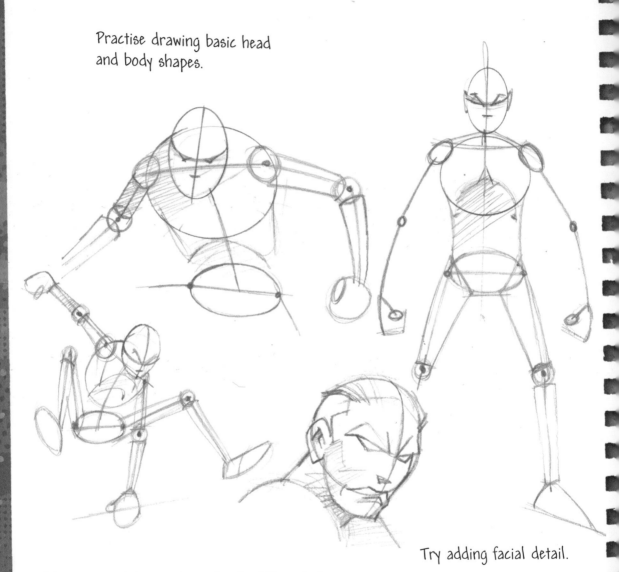

Try adding facial detail.

It's important to experiment with different shapes
and movements so that you gain experience. Look
at examples of manga to see how other artists in
the medium have handled the human form.

More quick sketches

Try experimenting
with different
characters.

Perspective

Perspective is a way of drawing objects so that they look as though they have three dimensions. Note how the part that is closest to you looks larger, and the part furthest away from you looks smaller. That's just how things look in real life.

The vanishing point (V.P.) is the place in a perspective drawing where parallel lines appear to meet. The position of the vanishing point depends on the viewer's eye level.

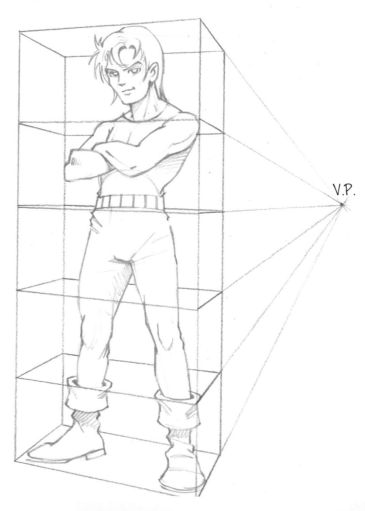

V.P.

Two-point perspective drawing

Two-point perspective uses two vanishing points: one for lines running along the length of the subject, and one on the opposite side for lines running across the width of the subject.

In this drawing the vanishing points are very low. This gives the impression that you are looking up at the figure – very dramatic!

Low eye level
(view from below)

V.P.

V.P.

High eye level
(view from above)

Three-point perspective adds a third vanishing point above or below the drawing (right).

V.P.

V.P.

V.P. = vanishing point

13

Materials

Pencils
Try out different grades of pencils. Hard pencils make fine grey lines and soft pencils make softer, darker marks.

Erasers
are useful for cleaning up drawings and removing construction lines.

Paper
Bristol paper is good for crayons, pastels and felt-tip pens. Watercolour paper is thicker; it is the best choice for water-based paints or inks.

Remember, the best equipment and materials will not necessarily make the best drawing – only practise will.

Use this sandpaper block if you want to shape your pencil to a really sharp point.

Inks

Use coloured inks straight from the bottle or dilute them with water.

Felt-tip pens

Felt-tips usually come in sets of mixed colours. The ones that make very thin lines are called fineliners.

Ink

Mixing palette

Fineliners

Dip-in pen nibs

Brushes

Correction fluid

Gouache

Watercolours

Technical drawing pens

Pens

Technical drawing pens have cartridges which can be refilled or replaced. Old-fashioned dip-in pens are much cheaper and come in many different styles and sizes.

Paints

Ordinary watercolours are translucent (see-through); gouache is not. Try other kinds of paints, too.

Styles

Try different types of drawing papers and materials. Experiment with pens, from felt-tips to ballpoints. They will make interesting marks. What happens if you draw with pen and ink on wet paper?

Silhouette is a style of drawing which mainly relies on solid dark shapes.

Felt-tips

come in a range of line widths.
The wider pens are good for
filling in large areas of flat tone.

17

Styles continued

Pencil

drawings can include a vast amount of detail and tone. Try different grades of pencil to get a range of light and shade effects in your drawings.

Lines drawn in **ink** cannot be erased, so unless you are very confident you may want to sketch your drawing in pencil first.

Hatching   Cross-hatching

It can be tricky adding light and shade to a drawing with a pen. Use a solid layer of ink for the very darkest areas and cross-hatching (straight lines criss-crossing each other) for ordinary dark tones. Use hatching (straight lines running parallel to each other) for midtones.

Body proportions

Heads in manga are drawn slightly bigger than in real life. Legs and hips make up more than half the overall height of the figure.

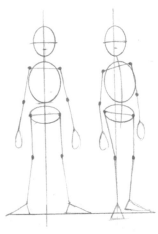

Drawing a stick figure is the simplest way to make decisions about a pose. It helps you see how different positions can change the centre of balance.

Use points to identify joints such as knees and elbows, so when you add detail to your character these will be in proportion.

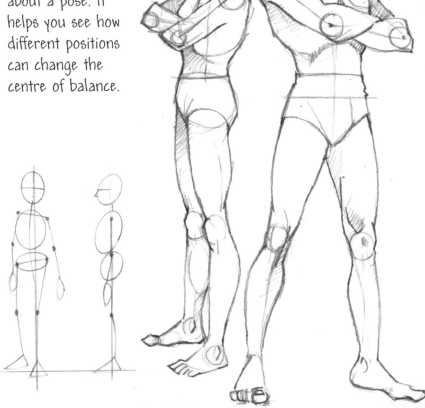

You often see heroes in dramatic poses. Experiment with poses like this.

Drawing a stick figure is the simplest way to make decisions about a pose. It helps you see how different positions can change the centre of balance.

Proportions

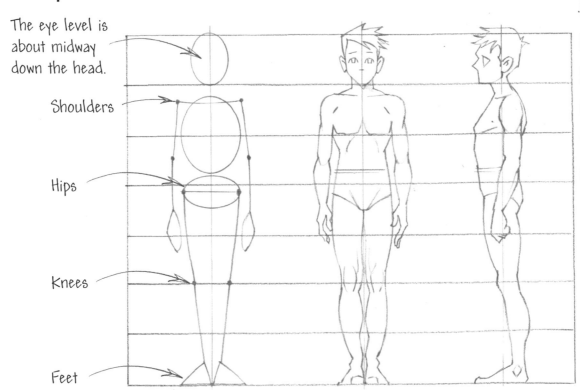

The eye level is about midway down the head.

Shoulders

Hips

Knees

Feet

Inking

Here's one way of inking over your final pencil drawing. Different tones of ink can be used to add depth to the drawing. Mix ink with water to achieve the tones you need.

Refillable inking pens come in various tip sizes. The tip is what determines the width of the line that is drawn. Sizes include: 0.1, 0.5, 1.0, 2.0 mm.

Correction fluid usually comes in small bottles or in pen format. This can be useful for cleaning up ink lines.

Different tones of ink can be used to add depth to the drawing. Mix ink with water to achieve the tones you need.

Heads

Manga heads have a distinctive style and shape. Drawing different facial expressions is very important – it shows instantly what your character is thinking or feeling.

1. Start by drawing a square. Fit the head, chin and neck inside it to keep the correct proportions. Draw two construction lines to position the top of the ear and the base of the nose.

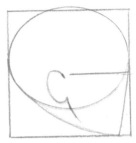

2. Add an oversized manga-style eye and draw the mouth and nose.

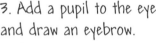

3. Add a pupil to the eye and draw an eyebrow.

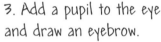

4. Draw some manga-style hair.

1. Draw a circle. Add construction lines through its centre point.

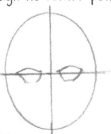

2. Using the construction lines, position the eyes, ears and mouth.

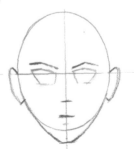

3. Then draw them in.

4. Draw the hair.

To create a head from the front, draw a rectangle and add the centrelines. Then add the oval shape of the head. Position the eyes, nose and mouth using the centrelines as a guide. Finally add ears and extra facial details.

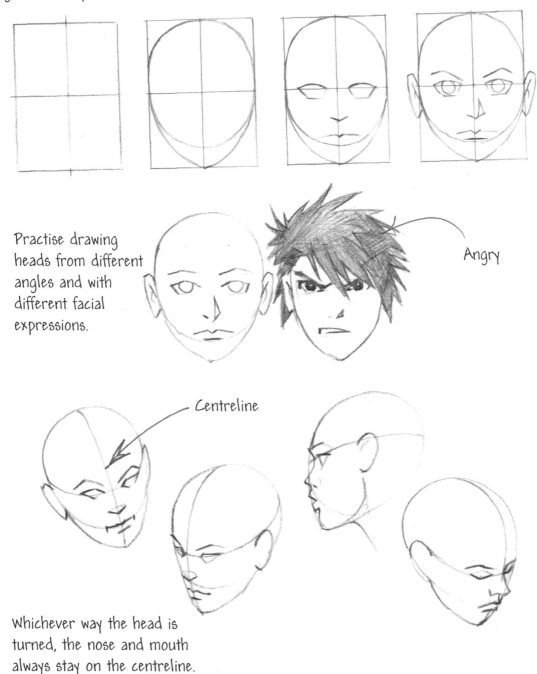

Practise drawing heads from different angles and with different facial expressions.

Angry

Centreline

Whichever way the head is turned, the nose and mouth always stay on the centreline.

Heads continued

Practise drawing heads from different angles and with different facial expressions.

Whichever way the head is turned, the nose and mouth always stay on the centre line.

Centre line

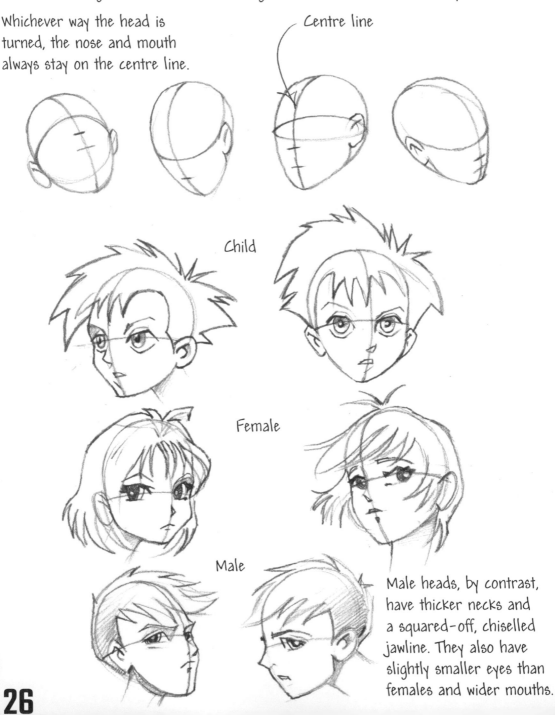

Child

Female

Male

Male heads, by contrast, have thicker necks and a squared-off, chiselled jawline. They also have slightly smaller eyes than females and wider mouths.

Light sources

The light source for your subject will change how you add shade to your drawing. Stark contrasts in light and shade can create dramatic effects in your image.

The shaded areas of an object are determined by the direction of the light source.

Here is a human head divided into sections to show how light from different sources effects the different areas of the head.

Light from above left

Light from above right

Light from below left

Light from below right

Creases and folds

Clothes fall into natural creases and folds when worn. Look at real people to see how fabric drapes and how it falls into creases. This will help you to dress your characters more realistically.

Creases occur where excess fabric gathers in folds. Drawing creases in clothing at joints will make your picture look more lifelike.

Clothes will hang and crease differently depending on the material.

Tight fitting

Medium fitting

Loose fitting

Drawing from life can help you understand where and why creases and folds occur.

The way fabric is drawn can instantly give a sense of movement and action to a pose.

Shading clothes is also very important. Think of all the places the light won't reach, such as inside trouser legs.

Characters

Hiro

Hiro is the king of the warriors. He is young, reckless and very brave. His samurai swords have magical powers, and were left to him by his ancient master.

1. Draw ovals for the head, body and hips. Add centre lines to divide the head vertically and horizontally. These will help you to place the ears and the nose.

Sketch an outline for Hiro's sword.

2. Add lines for the spine and the angle of the hips and shoulders.

Gradually build up long hair like this by adding wisps.

3. Draw stick arms and legs, with dots where the joints are. Add outline shapes for hands and feet.

These little circles are to remind you where the elbows and knees go.

4. Using the construction lines as a guide, start to build up the main shapes and features.

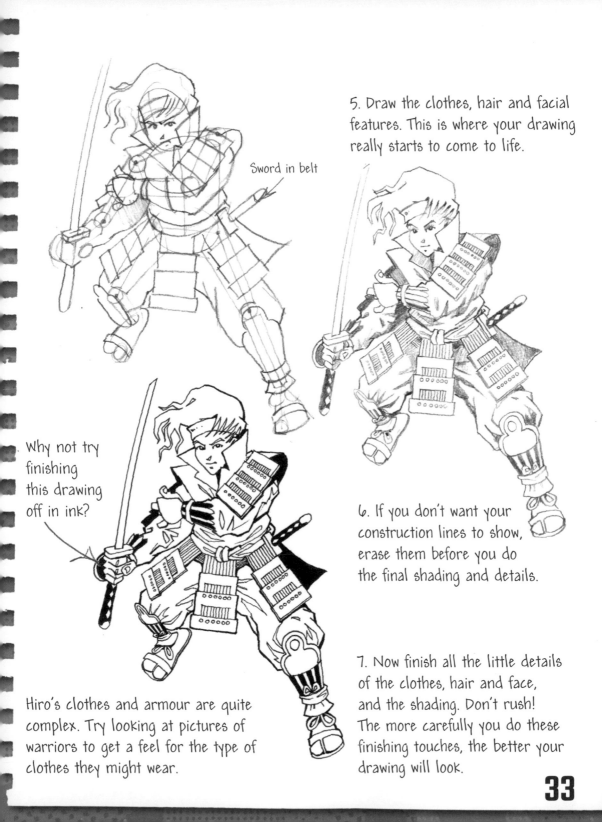

Sword in belt

5. Draw the clothes, hair and facial features. This is where your drawing really starts to come to life.

Why not try finishing this drawing off in ink?

6. If you don't want your construction lines to show, erase them before you do the final shading and details.

7. Now finish all the little details of the clothes, hair and face, and the shading. Don't rush! The more carefully you do these finishing touches, the better your drawing will look.

Hiro's clothes and armour are quite complex. Try looking at pictures of warriors to get a feel for the type of clothes they might wear.

Wokou captain

Terrifying pirates, the Wokou are feared among sailors everywhere. When the Captain draws his sword his enemies cower in fear.

Add a line for the sword.

1. Draw ovals for the head, body and hips. Add centrelines to divide the head vertically and horizontally.

2. Add lines for the spine and the angle of the hips and shoulders.

Position the ears, nose and mouth.

3. Draw stick arms and legs, with dots where the joints are. Add outline shapes for hands and feet.

4. Using the construction lines as a guide, start to build up the main shapes and features.

Draw little circles for the elbows and knees.

5. Draw the clothes, hair and facial features. This is where your drawing really starts to come to life.

6. Use shading to add detail to the clothing and sword. Adding detail like creases in clothes can make your characters more realistic.

7. If you don't want your construction lines to show, erase them before you do the final shading and details.

8. Now finish all the little details such as the shading on the hair and clothes. Don't rush! The more carefully you do these finishing touches, the better your drawing will look.

Instead of shading your drawing you can try finishing your drawing in ink. Go over all outlines in ink and remove any pencil lines.

Space boy

Space boy flies in zero gravity toward us in his specially modified space suit with power gauntlets.

1. Draw a circle for the head and ovals for the body and hips.

2. Add lines for the spine and the angle of the hips and shoulders.

3. Draw stick arms and legs with dots for the joints and shapes for the hands and feet.

4. Use your guidelines to sketch in the neck, facial features and hair.

Small circles indicate the positions of elbows and knees.

5. Using the construction lines as a guide, start drawing in the main shapes of the body.

Think about perspective here. Use front-end perspective to make the head and shoulders bigger and the legs and feet smaller—this way it looks like space boy is coming right at us!

6. Now start to sketch out the final shapes of clothes, hair, arms and legs.

Think about little details of space boy's power gauntlets and boots.

7. If you don't want your construction lines to show, erase them carefully before you add the finishing touches: shading, facial features, patterns on the clothes.

Finished off in ink

Mighty warrior

This mighty warrior hides his face with a horned mask while defeating his enemies with his immense strength and power.

1. Draw a circle for the head, and ovals for the body and hips.

2. Add lines for the spine and the angle of the hips and shoulders.

Add lines for the fingers.

3. Draw stick arms and legs with dots for the joints.

4. Use your guidelines to sketch in the facial features.

Draw little circles for the elbows and knees.

Draw in the fingers. Remember that due to perspective they appear very large as they are closer to us.

5. Using the construction lines as a guide, start drawing in the main shapes of the body.

Add the axe.

6. Draw in the finished shape of the figure, paying attention to the perspective of the arm and hand reaching out.

7. Now start to add details to his armour and cape.

8. If you don't want your construction lines to show, erase them carefully before you add the finishing touches.

Add shading to all the areas light wouldn't reach.

Go over the main outlines in ink and then erase the pencil drawing underneath for a different outcome.

The sorceress

The sorceress is very powerful and knows all the secrets of the earth. She keeps bad spirits away and can turn enemies to stone.

1. Draw ovals for the head and body.

2. Add lines for the spine and the angle of the shoulders.

3. Draw stick arms with dots for the joints and shapes for the hands.

4. Using your construction lines, sketch in the facial features and hair shape.

Put it in perspective! This hand is closest to us, therefore it is much bigger.

5. Flesh out the arms, legs and body, and add more detail to the face. Sketch the basic outline of the sorceress's wand.

6. Draw the shapes of the billowing hair and cloak. The facial expression should be dramatic but smiling.

Flyaway hair creates a dramatic effect and gives the impression of movement and wind.

7. Erase your construction lines if you don't want them to show.

8. Take plenty of time to finish the details of the face and hair, the cloak and the wand.

Long, elegant fingers help to give her character.

Shading shows which way her cloak and hair are blowing.

Wood detail on the wand.

If you want a different final look to your drawing you can try finishing it in ink. Carefully go over any outlines, and then remove any leftover pencil lines with an eraser.

Sorcerer

The sorcerer's powerful spells strike fear in many. He dreams of one day ruling the world.

1. Draw ovals for the head, body and hips. Add centrelines to divide the head horizontally.

2. Add lines for the spine and the angle of the hips and shoulders.

3. Draw stick arms and legs with dots where the joints are. Add outline shapes for hands and feet.

Sketch in the position of the sorcerer's book of spells.

Add a line for the staff.

Draw circles for the position of the shoulders, elbows and knees.

Add the basic facial features.

4. Using your construction lines as a guide, add the main shapes and features of the figure.

5. Draw the clothes, hair and facial features.

Adding details like fringes on his jacket and an intricate belt buckle help bring the character to life.

6. Sketch in the sorcerer's many accessories.

7. Erase your construction lines if you don't want them to show.

8. Take plenty of time to finish the details of the face and body, adding shading to areas where light wouldn't reach.

You could try finishing your drawing in ink.

43

Dragon girl

Dragon girl possesses magic cards which can unleash the power of various mighty dragons.

1. Draw different-sized ovals for the head, body and hips. This time, add another oval for the dragon's head.

2. Add a line for the spine and others to show the angle of the hips and shoulders.

Add the dragon's open mouth.

Magic card

3. Draw stick arms and legs with dots for the joints and outline shapes for the hands.

4. Using your construction lines as a guide, draw the main shapes of the body and the position of the facial features.

5. Add detail to the face, hair and costume of dragon girl. Build up the features of the dragon as you go along.

Add movement lines to this dramatic pose.

6. Erase the construction lines if you want to, then finish off all remaining details and add shading.

Practise drawing hands gripping objects.

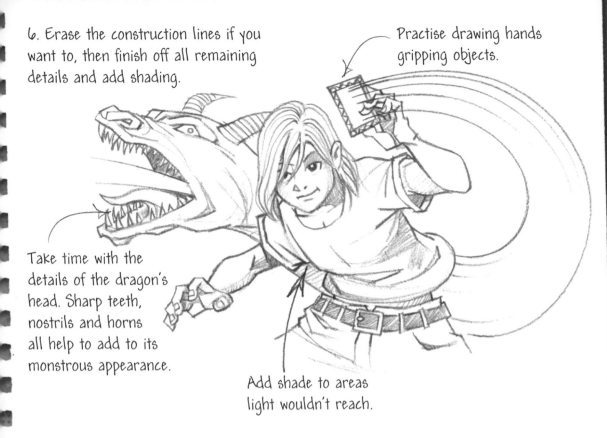

Take time with the details of the dragon's head. Sharp teeth, nostrils and horns all help to add to its monstrous appearance.

Add shade to areas light wouldn't reach.

Instead of shading your drawing you can try finishing your drawing in ink. Go over all outlines in ink and remove any pencil lines.

The pose of dragon girl creates folds and creases in her clothes. Think about how to shade these areas.

45

Yakuza

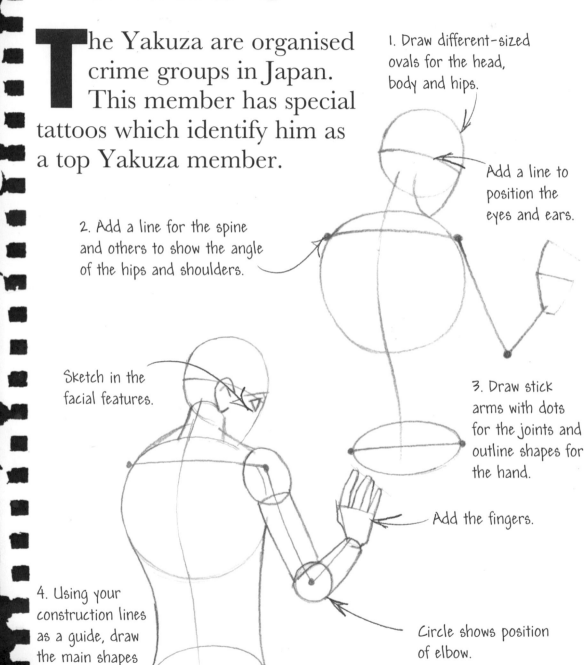

The Yakuza are organised crime groups in Japan. This member has special tattoos which identify him as a top Yakuza member.

1. Draw different-sized ovals for the head, body and hips.

Add a line to position the eyes and ears.

2. Add a line for the spine and others to show the angle of the hips and shoulders.

Sketch in the facial features.

3. Draw stick arms with dots for the joints and outline shapes for the hand.

Add the fingers.

4. Using your construction lines as a guide, draw the main shapes of the body.

Circle shows position of elbow.

5. Draw in more detail to the face and hair. Add more form to the body and begin to sketch out the tattoo.

6. Erase the construction lines if you want to and finish off all the remaining details.

Sunglasses give a mysterious look.

Don't forget to add details like his belt.

You can try finishing your drawing in ink.

Ninja

Moving silently through the night, the ninja is the master of stealth, spying on people unnoticed.

1. Draw circles for the head and body and an oval for the hips. Sketch lines for the spine and the angles of the hips and shoulders, with dots to position the joints.

2. Draw stick arms and legs, with basic shapes for the hands and feet.

3. Now start to outline the arms, legs and torso. Add some facial features. Remember, eyes and ears are always on the centre line!

This is a strong hero pose. Look at pictures of martial arts masters to get an idea of how the legs should bend.

Draw circles for knees and elbows.

Don't forget to use your construction lines as a guide when drawing the basic shapes of the body.

4. Now sketch in the basic shapes of the clothes and mask. Think about how the robes will crease at the knees, chest and groin.

We cannot see the other arm, but use construction lines to ensure the hand is proportioned correctly.

Three fingers up

Trousers are tied just below the knee.

Belt detail

5. Erase your construction lines and take your time to finish all the details, like the folds and shading in the clothes.

The ninja looks great finished off in ink. Try drawing her in silhouette, too!

49

Princess Aku

Aku is Japanese for 'evil', and this princess certainly lives up to her name.

1. Draw different-sized ovals for the hips, body and head.

2. Draw stick arms and legs in a sitting position, with dots for the joints. Sketch in simple shapes for the feet.

3. Draw in the main shape of the body, using the ovals to guide you.

Begin to sketch the outline of the opulent throne.

4. Add details to the head, defining the shape of the facial features and hair. Begin to add detail to the robes and throne.

Drape robes over the throne.

5. Erase your construction lines and take your time to finish all the details.

Add the complex tiara and strands of hair.

Draw in the high shoulder pads and folds of the costume.

Add shading to areas where light wouldn't reach.

Finish the details of the feet, adding sandals.

If you want a different final look to your drawing you can try finishing it in ink. Carefully go over any outlines and then erase any leftover pencil lines with an eraser.

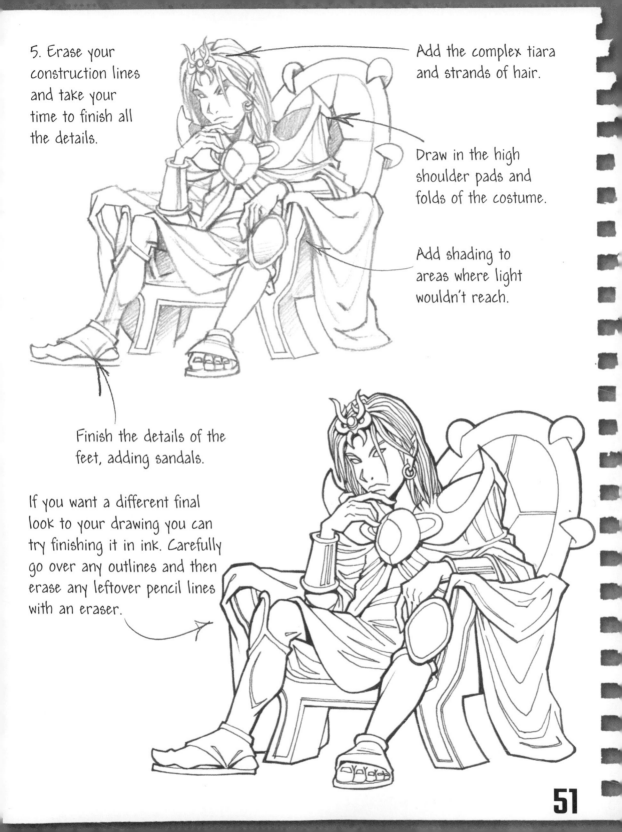

Monkey

Monkey is young, brash and very brave. He is rebellious and will break any rules to help fight crime and save people. He can swing from rooftop to rooftop.

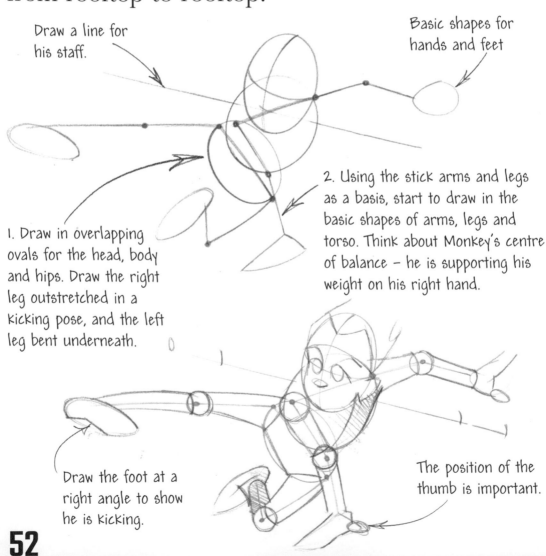

Draw a line for his staff.

Basic shapes for hands and feet

2. Using the stick arms and legs as a basis, start to draw in the basic shapes of arms, legs and torso. Think about Monkey's centre of balance – he is supporting his weight on his right hand.

1. Draw in overlapping ovals for the head, body and hips. Draw the right leg outstretched in a kicking pose, and the left leg bent underneath.

Draw the foot at a right angle to show he is kicking.

The position of the thumb is important.

3. Start drawing the details, such as the clothes, hair and facial features.

Drawing the hair like this gives the impression he is moving very fast!

Monkey tail

This is a good picture to practise drawing creases and folds. There are lots of creases because Monkey is moving fast.

4. Erase construction lines before adding final details.

Try adding little details like the headgear.

Larger eyes with highlights let us know Monkey is a child.

Highlights in the hair.

Here's the same drawing finished in ink. Remove any leftover pencil lines.

Mad scientist

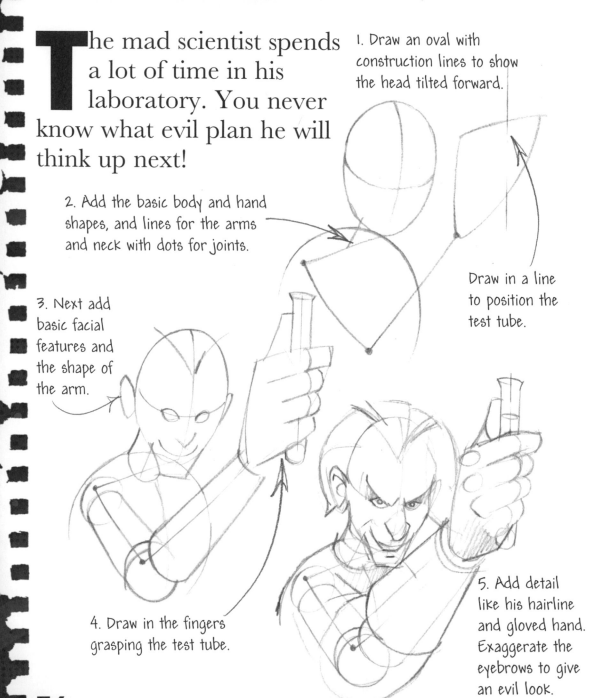

The mad scientist spends a lot of time in his laboratory. You never know what evil plan he will think up next!

1. Draw an oval with construction lines to show the head tilted forward.

2. Add the basic body and hand shapes, and lines for the arms and neck with dots for joints.

Draw in a line to position the test tube.

3. Next add basic facial features and the shape of the arm.

4. Draw in the fingers grasping the test tube.

5. Add detail like his hairline and gloved hand. Exaggerate the eyebrows to give an evil look.

6. Finish the head by adding details such as messy hair and eyebrows.

7. Erase construction lines before adding final details such as shading and the highlights in the eyes.

Add liquid inside the test tube.

Add shaded areas to show the creases in the rubber glove.

Leave areas blank or erase back to white for highlights.

Here's the same drawing finished in ink. Decide which lines you want to ink in before you make any marks.

55

Robo-captain

The robo-captain is half man, half machine and he comes from the future. He is invincible, he can fly and he protects everyone from danger. Everyone's safe when the captain's around!

We won't see the facial features in the finished picture, but it is still important to position them.

1. Draw the ovals and construction lines for a basic standing pose. Remember, draw stick arms and legs with dots for joints.

Basic shapes for hands and feet

2. Sketch the arms and legs. This is a good, solid hero pose. Drawing the fists clenched will add drama to the figure.

Add circles for knees, elbows and shoulders.

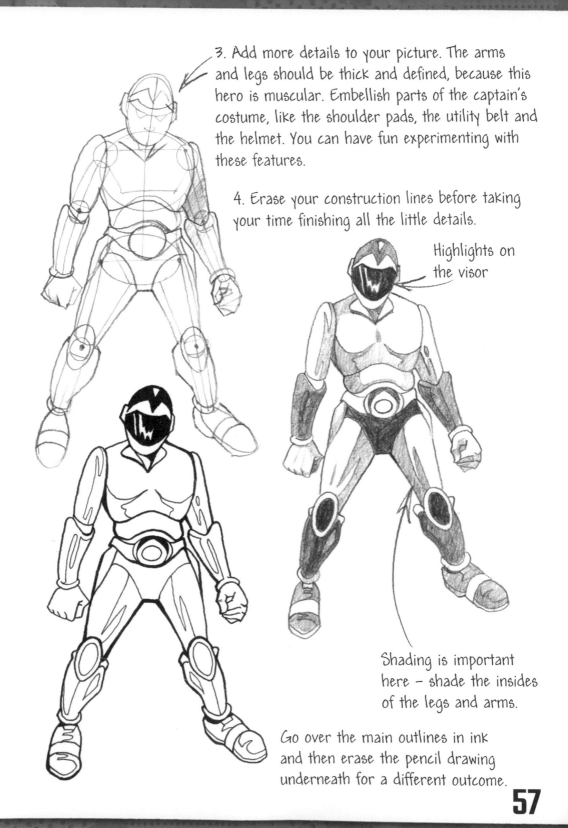

3. Add more details to your picture. The arms and legs should be thick and defined, because this hero is muscular. Embellish parts of the captain's costume, like the shoulder pads, the utility belt and the helmet. You can have fun experimenting with these features.

4. Erase your construction lines before taking your time finishing all the little details.

Highlights on the visor

Shading is important here – shade the insides of the legs and arms.

Go over the main outlines in ink and then erase the pencil drawing underneath for a different outcome.

Tero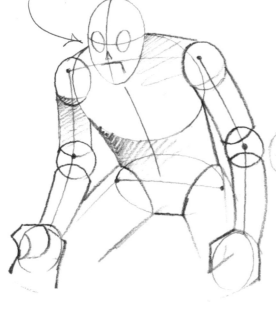

Tero possesses super-human strength. He often struggles to keep his temper under control.

1. Draw the basic ovals and construction lines. Add dots where the joints will be.

2. Use your construction lines to add details to the limbs. Add the basic shape of the mask.

Sketch in the hair.

3. Using the construction line framework, define the body shape. Add a jacket and fingers to the hands.

4. Complete the detail of the mask, muscles and jacket.

Draw in the hair using jagged lines.

Ripped clothes suggests frightening strength.

5. Add shading to suggest muscle tone.

Add detail to the hand. Clenched fists indicate anger and strength.

You can try finishing your drawing in ink.

Glossary

Armour Protective clothing that is worn into battle.

Composition The positioning of the various parts of a picture on the drawing paper.

Construction lines Guidelines used in the early stages of a drawing which are usually erased later.

Cross-hatching A series of criss-crossing lines used to add shade to a drawing.

Dragon Mythical creatures with scaly skin, wings, a long tail and the ability to breathe fire.

Gauntlet An armoured glove.

Hatching A series of parallel lines used to add shade to a drawing.

Manga A Japanese word for 'comic' or 'cartoon'; also the style of drawing that is used in Japanese comics.

Ninjas Secret agents in feudal Japan who used stealth and martial arts to carry out assassinations and other acts of covert warfare.

Pirates Criminals who operate at sea, boarding ships to take crews hostage and steal their cargo.

Proportions The size of each part of something in relation to the whole.

Samurai Members of the warrior class in Japanese society in the medieval and early-modern periods.

Sandals Light shoes where the sole is attached to the foot by straps.

Silhouette A drawing that shows only a dark shape, like a shadow, sometimes with details left white.

Three-dimensional Having an effect of depth, so as to look like a real character rather than a flat picture of a character.

Tone The contrast between light and shade that helps to add depth to a picture.

Vanishing point The place in a perspective drawing where parallel lines appear to meet.

Visor The part of a helmet or other piece of headgear that protects the eyes.

Wand A long stick or rod, associated with casting magic spells in folklore and fantasy literature.

Index